INTRODUCTION

Why did you buy this book, too?

You bought it because you love learning about the ukulele. And we're glad—it's a great instrument!

We assume that you've already completed (and reviewed a couple hundred times) **FastTrack®** **Ukulele 1** (HL00114417). If not, please consider going through it first. (We'd hate to cover something before you're ready.)

In any case, this book picks up right where **Book 1** ended. You'll learn lots more chords, more notes, and plenty of cool techniques. And, of course, the last two songs in all the **FastTrack®** books are the same so that you and your friends can form a band and jam together!

So, if you still feel ready for this book, finish your pizza, put the dog outside, turn off your phone, and let's jam...

Always remember the three **P**s: **P**atience, **P**ractice and **P**ace yourself. We'll add one more to this list: be **P**roud of yourself for a job well-done!

ABOUT THE AUDIO

We're glad you noticed the added bonus—online audio tracks! Each music example in the book is included, so you can hear how it sounds and play along when you're ready. Take a listen whenever you see this symbol:

Each audio example is preceded by count-off "clicks" to indicate the tempo and meter. Pan right to hear the ukulele part emphasized. Pan left to hear the accompaniment emphasized. As you become more confident, try playing along with the rest of the band. (Remember to use Track 1 to help you tune before you play.)

To access audio visit:
www.halleonard.com/mylibrary

Enter Code
8648-4004-8345-9479

ISBN 978-1-5400-2629-3

HAL•LEONARD®

Copyright © 2019 by HAL LEONARD LLC
International Copyright Secured   All Rights Reserved

Visit Hal Leonard Online at
www.halleonard.com

Contact us:
Hal Leonard
7777 West Bluemound Road
Milwaukee, WI 53213
Email: info@halleonard.com

In Europe, contact:
Hal Leonard Europe Limited
42 Wigmore Street
Marylebone, London, W1U 2RN
Email: info@halleonardeurope.com

In Australia, contact:
Hal Leonard Australia Pty. Ltd.
4 Lentara Court
Cheltenham, Victoria, 3192 Australia
Email: info@halleonard.com.au

LESSON 1
Got blues?

Let's begin with something fun and simple—the 12-bar blues! This is a song form or chord progression (it's both!) that's very common in blues, rock, country, pop... you name it! From Chuck Berry's "Johnny B. Goode" to Stevie Ray Vaughan's "Pride and Joy," you've no doubt heard the 12-bar blues form countless times. What's better is that it sounds great on the uke! So, let's get started...

The I, IV and V Chords

In **Book 1**, we learned a lot of chords, but we didn't really talk about keys. A song's **key** is the note or chord that feels like "home." Often, the first and/or last chord in a song will be the home (or **tonic**) chord (but not always). In a key, we label the chords using Roman numerals—uppercase for major chords and lowercase for minor chords. The three chords used in the 12-bar blues form are the I, IV and V chords. In the key of C, that's C major, F major and G major.

Let's play a 12-bar blues progression using a shuffle feel.

◆ Learnin' the Blues

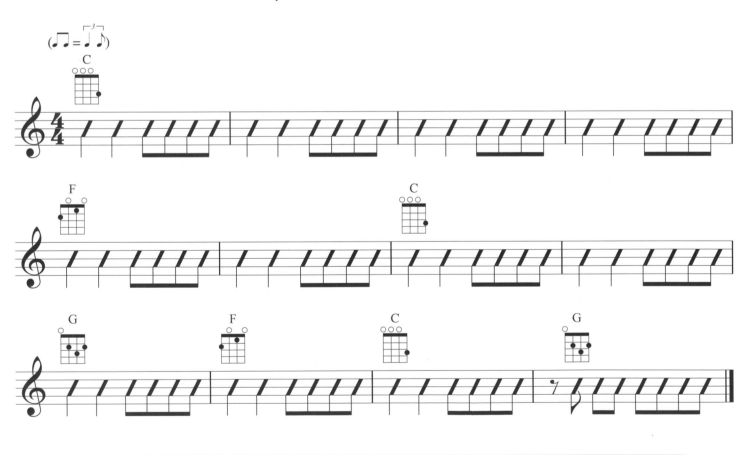

☞ There are many variations of this 12-bar form, as we'll soon see!

Get a little more "down-home"...

To make it sound even bluesier, you can play all dominant seventh chords instead of just major chords. You already know C7 and G7 from **Book 1**, so let's learn the other chord: F7.

F7 Chord

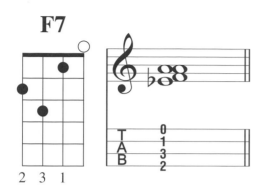

Now, let's put these seventh chords to work! This time we'll use a common variation of the form called the "quick change." This means, instead of beginning with four measures on the I chord, we'll change to the IV chord in measure 2 and then go back to the I chord in measure 3.

❸ Dominant Blues

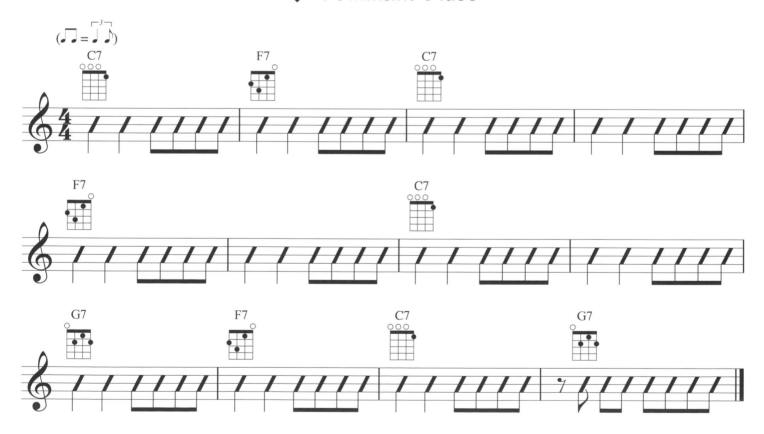

Take a solo!

Ready to step into the spotlight? Let's play a solo over this 12-bar blues using notes we learned in **Book 1**. Turn the page and start jamming!

◆ Blues Solo

Changing it up!

Now that you have a good grasp of the blues form in C, let's try another key. We can play a blues form in G using chords we learned in **Book 1**: G7 (the I chord), C7 (the IV chord) and D7 (the V chord). We'll change up the strumming pattern a bit here to keep it interesting.

⑤ Blues in G

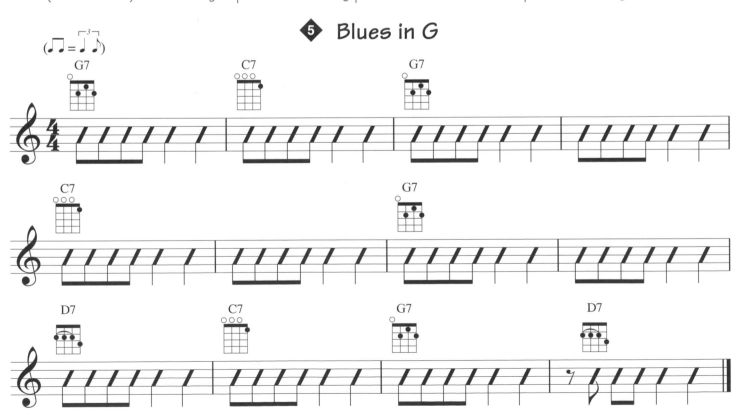

LET'S BOOGIE

Another fun blues concept is the "boogie woogie" style. This style was famously adapted from piano to guitar, and now we can adapt it to the uke. We'll go back to the key of C for this one.

The idea is to play two-note chord forms in which one note (the root of the chord) stays constant while the top notes alternate. The base form is called a **power chord** (indicated by "5" in the chord name), which is built from a root and a 5th. (Don't worry about understanding why it's a 5th. Just trust us!) Here are the power chord forms we'll use for C, F and G:

C5 Chord

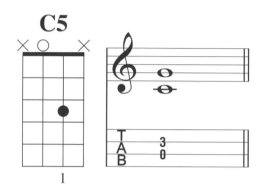

F5 Chord

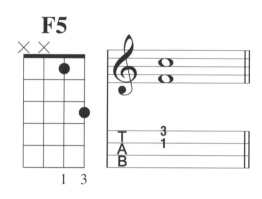

G5 Chord

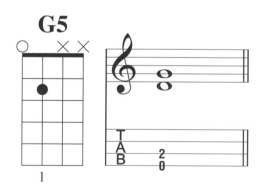

> 👉 NOTE: Because of the uke's reentrant tuning, the G5 chord is the oddball.
> The chord's root note (G) actually sounds higher than the 5th. That's ok, though—
> it still sounds great!

To play the boogie, we alternate each chord's 5th with a note that's a whole step (two frets) higher. Since this note is the 6th of the chord, you sometimes see this two-note form called C6 (or F6, etc.). For example, we'll alternate this C5 chord form:

with this form:

And that's how we boogie! Let's try out our new C-chord boogie pattern:

◆ C-Chord Boogie

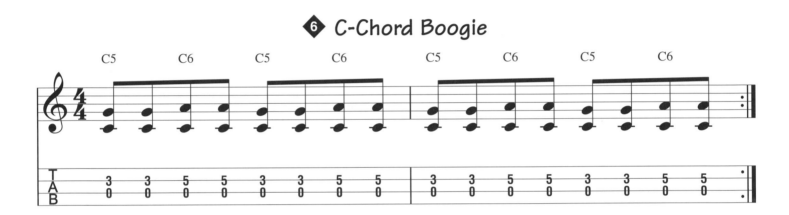

☞ NOTE: It's common to strum boogies with all downstrokes if the tempo's not too fast.

For a blues boogie, we do this for all three chords. Our F and G forms would look like this: (You have to stretch a bit with F, but you can do it!)

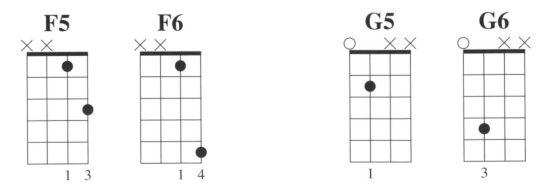

Let's jam!

Now, let's plug these into our 12-bar form and play a boogie blues in C. In measure 12, we'll abandon the boogie and resort to our G7 chord to goose it up a bit. Also notice that we've simplified the chord symbols—this is often done in boogies like these.

7 It's Boogie Time, You C

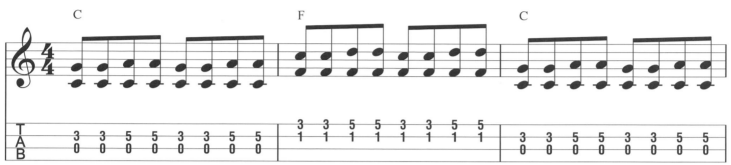

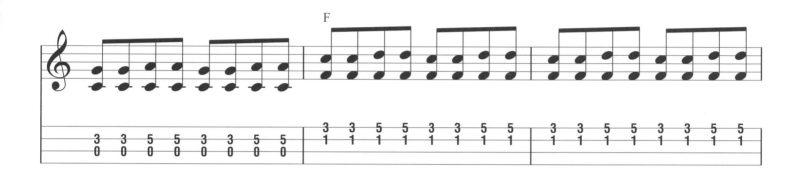

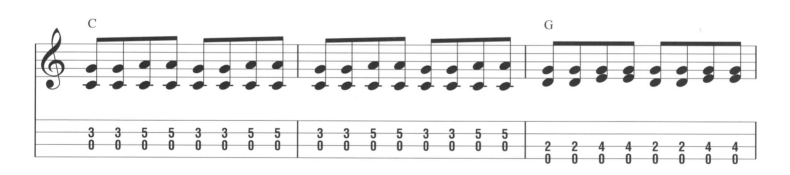

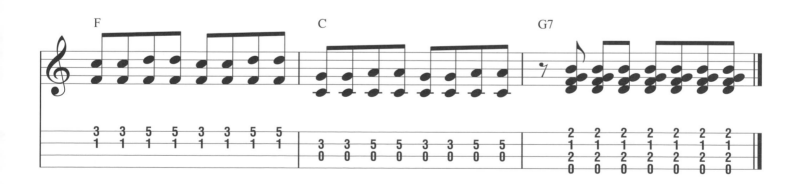

Kick it up a notch...

For a great-sounding variation on the boogie, we can add a note one fret higher for each chord (Thankfully, the frets are small on a uke!) TIP: For the F chord, remember that you don't have to hold down your ring finger when stretching with your pinky! Don't worry about what these notes are called right now; just take note of what's happening with each chord form.

8 ◆ Down-Home Boogie

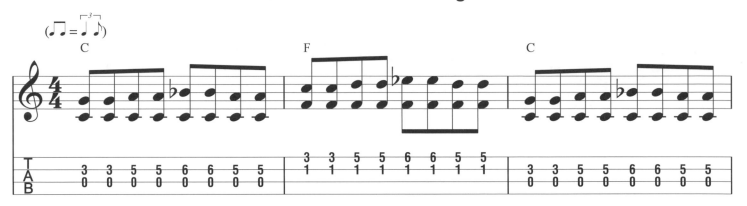

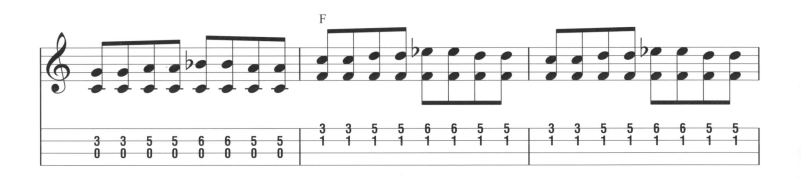

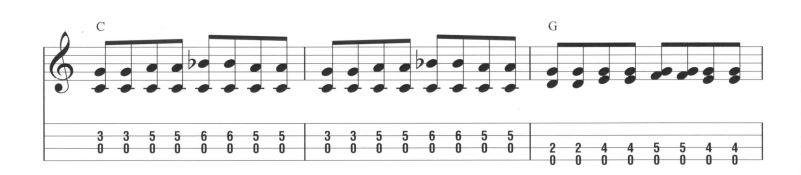

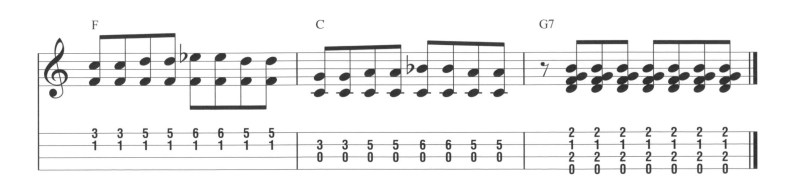

LESSON 2
Liven up your strumming...

There's no doubt that uke players love to strum. In this lesson, we're going to look at a few ways we can liven things up a bit. In **Book 1**, you learned about using downstrums and upstrums with a shuffle feel, and you built up an impressive chord vocabulary. Now, let's learn a few more new chords and some cool techniques to go with them!

Staccato

It may sound like an Italian pasta dish, but it can do wonders for your strumming. **Staccato** means "short" or "clipped." In music notation, it's indicated by a dot above or below the note head, and it tells you to clip the note or chord short. In other words, you don't allow it to ring for its full duration.

Take our trusty open C chord, for example. Try strumming it in quarter notes, immediately stopping each chord from ringing. It should sound like this:

You may have noticed that there are two ways to stop the chord from ringing: with your fret hand (laying an unused finger across the strings) or with your strumming hand (touching the strings with your palm). Chords that have open strings are a bit harder to play staccato because they require a little more effort to stop the strings from ringing.

By contrast, let's try the same thing using our A-form C barre chord, which you learned in **Book 1**:

You may have found this easier, because there's a little trick to it. Since there are no open strings—i.e., all the strings are fretted—you can simply release the fret-hand pressure to stop the chord from ringing. You don't have to use your strumming hand at all.

Let's jam!

When we mix staccato strums with normal strums, we can really add some flavor.

11 **Long and Short**

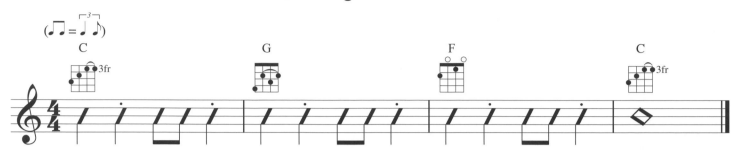

UP TO YOUR NECK IN CHORDS

In **Book 1**, you learned several moveable chord forms, all of which are based on open chords. In other words, an A-form chord looks like the open A chord; a C-form chord looks like the open C chord, etc. Let's quickly review these moveable forms. In all of these chord diagrams, the root will be circled.

Major Forms

A-form

C-form

D-form

F-form

Minor Forms

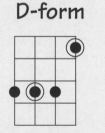

Am-form

Dm-form

Now, let's stick our neck out and try some of these forms while practicing our staccato technique. Remember to reference the chart on page 10 if you need to.

⑫ Bad Moon Rock

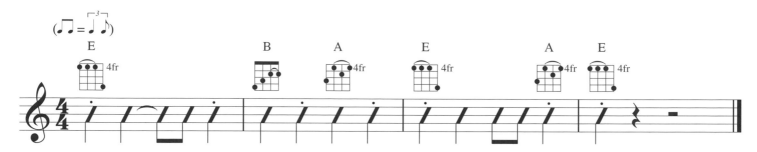

⑬ Majors and Minors

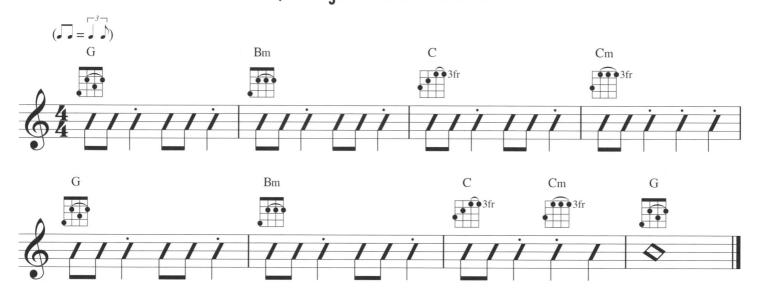

☞ HINT! Don't lift your barre finger if you don't have to! For example, when moving from the G chord to the Bm chord, you can just leave your index-finger barre where it is for both chords.

The rhythm is a little tricky in this one, so listen to the audio if you're having trouble with it.

⑭ Morse Code

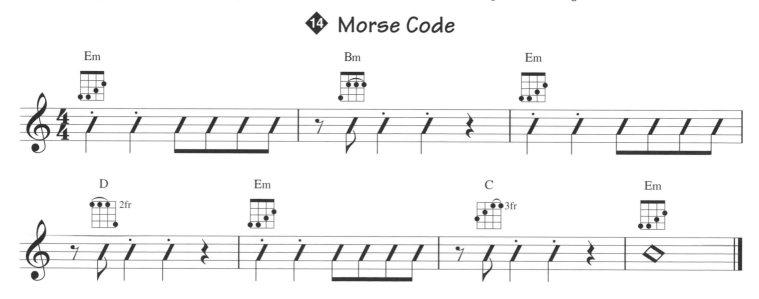

The tempo on this next one is a little slower, so you can use all downstrums. Lift your fret-hand fingers quickly for those staccato eighth notes!

🔶15 Australian Rock

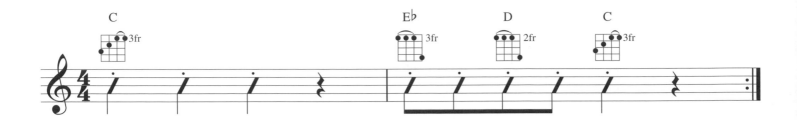

Bring out your dead!

Another way to add life to your strumming patterns is with **dead notes** or **dead strums**. (No, the irony didn't escape us!) The idea is simple. You simply touch the strings lightly—but don't push them down—and strum. This should create a purely rhythmic thud. Listen to track 18 to hear a demonstration.

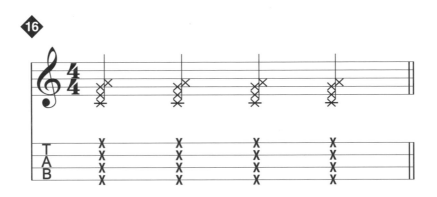

As with the staccato technique, this idea pairs really well with moveable chords, because your fingers are already covering all the strings. So, all you have to do is release the pressure (while still touching the strings), and you can play a dead strum.

Try it out with these C and Bb chords:

🔶17 Two-Chord Rock

By mixing in some eighth notes, you can create some great little grooves with this technique!

18 Dead Note Shuffle

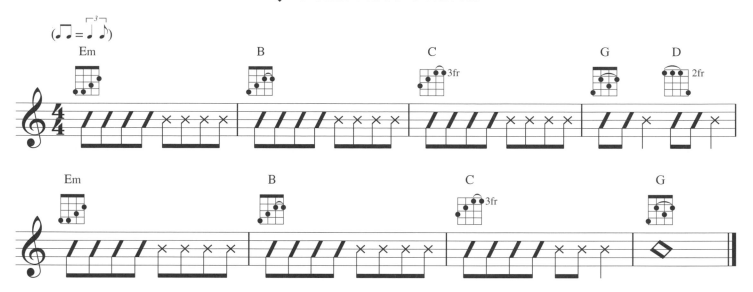

19 Reggae Rock

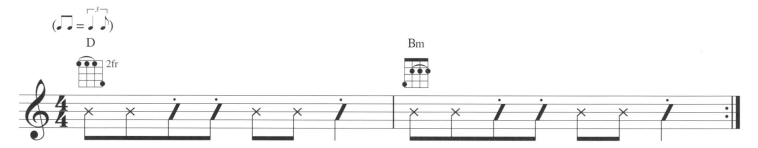

Let's try to sus things out...

It's time to add a new chord flavor to your arsenal: **sus chords**. Short for "suspended" chords, a sus chord is neither major nor minor. It's still a three-note chord (three different notes, that is), but the note that determines whether it's major or minor (which is the 3rd) has been replaced.

There are two types of sus chords: **sus2** and **sus4**. When played by themselves, they have a somewhat arid quality, but they also work great as decorations for a major or minor chord. Let's check out a few open **sus4** chords:

Asus4 Chord

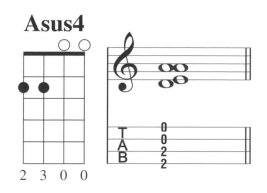

This one works great when alternated with A or Am. Two fingers are all you need!

Gsus4 Chord

Next up is Gsus4. Notice that there are two fingerings shown below the chord grid. What's up with that? Well, if you're going to be alternating this chord with a G major chord, you're better off using the top row of numbers. If you're alternating with G minor, the bottom row will work best. Try it out—you'll thank us!

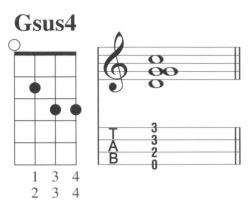

Csus4 Chord

This one is just like our F5 chord from page 5, only we're adding the open strings 4 and 3. Voila! Now it's a Csus4 chord.

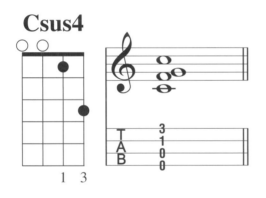

Dsus4 Chord

This one will be a relief when compared to the D major chord. Your fingers finally get a little wiggle room! Again, there are two fingerings shown. The top row is recommended, as you can easily alternate it with a D or Dm chord.

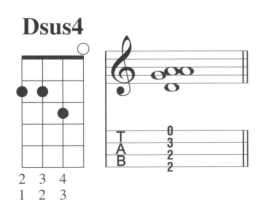

Let's take those brand-new sus chords out for a spin:

20 All Sussed Out

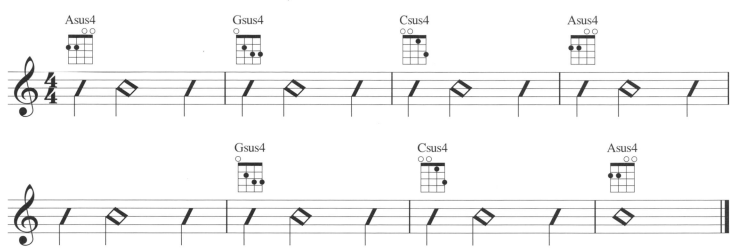

SYNCOPATION

No, this isn't a term for two people that have the same occupation. To **syncopate** means to stress a weaker beat. This is a great way to spice up your strum patterns, and you hear it all the time. (Seriously… all the time!)

In 4/4 meter, beats 1 and 3 are naturally stressed a bit more than beats 2 and 4. Likewise, all of the downbeats—i.e., the beats that you count "1, 2, 3, 4"—are naturally stressed more than the upbeats—i.e., the eighth-note "ands" between the beats.

The previous example actually introduced a bit of syncopation by accenting beat 2 with a half note. But we can heighten the effect by stressing an upbeat. Check out the next example to see what we mean. Notice that there are two different sets of strum directions. Try them both to see which feels better. The top row keeps your hand moving in a consistent down-and-up motion throughout, while the bottom row may make it easier to accent those weak beats, since downstrums generally tend to be stronger than upstrums.

The accents are reinforced in the music with the > symbol.

21 Syncopating and Sussing

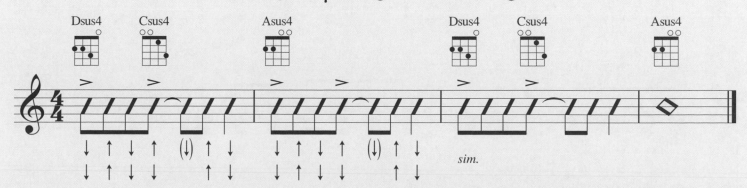

Be on the lookout for other syncopated patterns that crop up. But don't worry—when one is especially tricky, we'll be sure to provide some strum directions to help you out!

Let's try one in 3/4 meter. You remember 3/4 from **Book 1**, don't you? In this example, we're alternating sus4 chords with their major counterparts—a very common move!

22 Just Sussin' Around

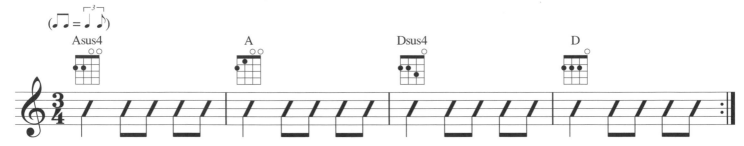

HINT! Always look for easy fingering solutions in chord progressions. In "Just Sussin' Around," for example, if you use your middle finger for fret 2, string 4, you can leave it there for all the chords!

You can make great little chord riffs with sus chords, too. We'll write this next one out in tab because it almost sounds more like a riff than a strum pattern.

23 Suspenseful

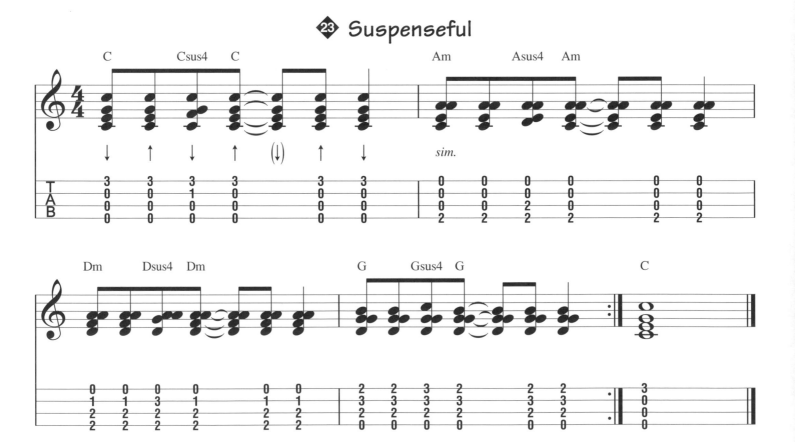

24 Ice Cold

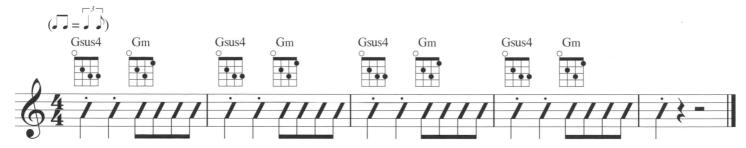

A DIFFERENT KIND OF DEAD

Remember how we mentioned that dead strums are easier with moveable chords because you don't have any open strings to worry about? Well, there's a way around that, and we're going to show it to you now. (You've been patient and a good sport, after all.) This is another way to create a dead strum that's solely created with your strumming hand, so it works well regardless of what chord you're playing.

Here's what you do. As you strum the strings with a downstrum, simultaneously bring your palm down on them to quiet them. You should get a percussive tick or thud. This sound is a combination of your strumming fingers making contact with the strings and your palm (or side of the hand) making contact at the same time.

Try it out with an open C chord to get the feel of it:

25

Once you've got the hang of it, try this sus riff:

26 A Petty Suspension

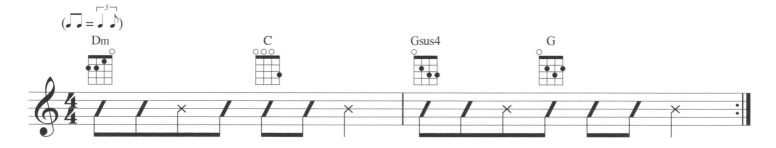

Combine this technique with the original dead strum (created by relaxing your fret-hand fingers) to cover just about any situation.

How about a few open **sus2** chords now?

Gsus2 Chord

There are two fingerings shown for this one. The top row works better for alternating with a G major chord, while the bottom row is better with a G minor chord.

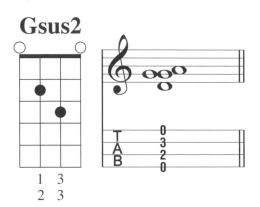

Dsus2 Chord

If this chord looks familiar, then you should be a detective, because you're absolutely right! You learned it earlier as Asus4.

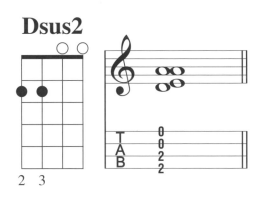

☞ TIP! Any sus4 chord can actually be named a sus2 from a different root and vice versa. It's kind of a sneaky music theory trick. Why is this so? Well, an Asus4 chord contains the notes A, D and E. A Dsus2 chord contains the same notes, only it considers D the root: D, E and A. The same can be said for Gsus4 (G-C-D) and Csus2 (C-D-G), and any other sus2 or sus4 chord! So, don't be surprised if you see a sus2 chord that looks like another sus4 chord.

Now let's try out these sneaky chords:

27 The Heart of the Sus Chord

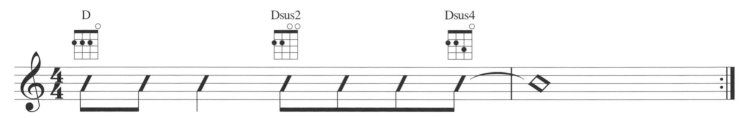

Be careful on this next one. We're changing chords an eighth note early each time!

28 To Sus or Not to Sus

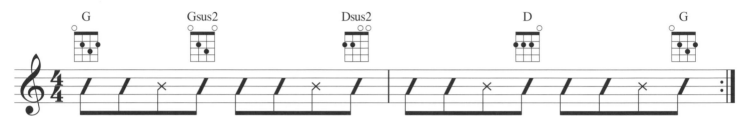

☞ TIP! Pay attention to the strumming directions. Keep your strumming hand moving steadily down and up, purposefully "missing" the strings when necessary.

29 Here a Sus, There a Sus

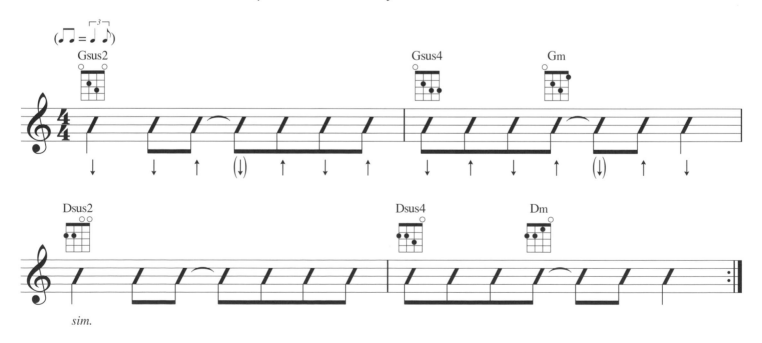

LESSON 3
Tipping the scales in your favor...

Now we're going to expand our knowledge and have fun doing it. (That's the whole point, right?) It's time to talk about scales. A **scale** is a sequence of notes based on a specific pattern of whole steps and half steps. (If you remember from **Book 1**, a half step is one fret on the uke, and a whole step is two frets.) Just like chords, scales can be major or minor.

ON THE GRID

Since you're so familiar with chord grids now, let's learn another shorthand form of notation: a **scale grid**. This is another graphical representation of the uke neck that's handy for writing out scale forms. Check it out:

C Major Scale

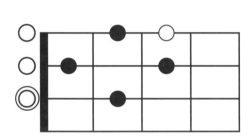
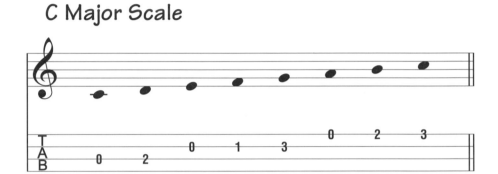

Above, you can see the scale grid on the left, followed by the same thing shown in standard notation and tab. The tonic notes (C, in this case) are indicated by an open circle on the scale grid.

On the move...

As with chord grids, when a scale is to be played up the neck and away from open position, the nut will not be visible, and a fret marker will indicate what frets the grid represents. Here's a D major scale represented on the grid, only this time in **moveable form**—i.e., using all fretted notes (no open strings). Note the "2fr" at the bottom, indicating that it begins at the second fret.

D Major Scale

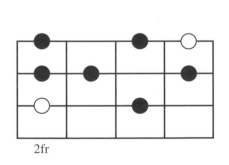
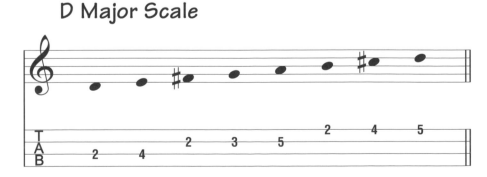

Congratulations—you just played your first moveable scale! Be sure to notice the following before heading out to celebrate:

 The scale "form"—i.e., the arrangement of dots on the scale grid—is exactly the same as for the C major scale. The only difference is that we've moved everything up the neck by two frets.

 If you haven't realized by now, this should help illustrate the fact that you can play most notes in many different places on the ukulele neck! For example, the open second string is the note E. That same note can be played at fret 4 on the third string.

Now, let's play a few melodies using these two scale forms: the open-position C major scale form and the moveable D major form. You can pluck these melodies with your thumb or index finger. (Some folks will alternate their index and middle fingers for speedier phrases.)

30 Stair-Steppin'

Notice that the rhythm in the next example is very similar to "Stair-Steppin'," only this time there are no rests, so the notes sustain. Details are important! (Who knew?)

31 Comin' Back Home

32 Tiptoeing

33 Pivot Lick

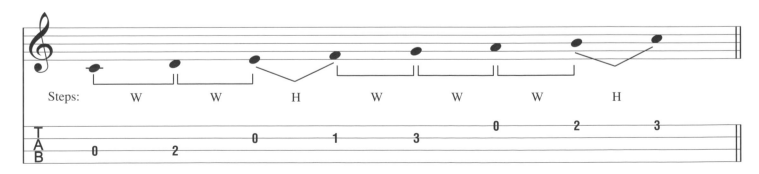

KEYS, PLEASE

A song's key is determined by the scale used to create the chords and melodies within it. In other words, if a song uses the C major scale for the chords and melodies, then the song is said to be "in the key of C." You learned a little about keys in Lesson 1, but now we'll dig a bit deeper.

The name game...

There are two things that give a scale its name: the tonic note (sometimes called "root note"), which is indicated on our grids with an open circle, and the pattern of whole-step and half-step intervals.

Let's look at the two most common scale patterns. This first one should look familiar!

Major Scale Pattern

Since C is our tonic, this is a C major scale.

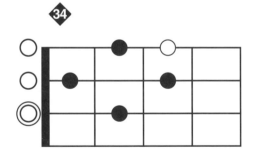

22

Minor Scale Pattern

Although C is still our tonic, the pattern of intervals has changed. This is a C minor scale.

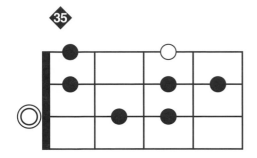

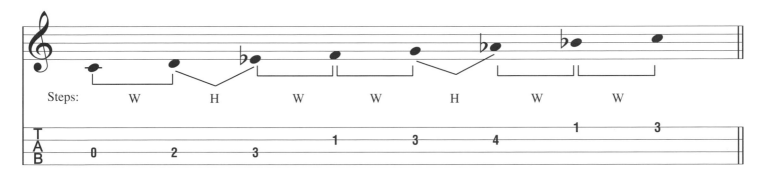

Steps: W   H   W   W   H   W   W

☞ TIP: Use your ear! Without checking the pattern, you can hear the difference between a major and minor scale. Just as with chords, a major scale sounds happy, and a minor scale sounds sad.

Some things are unavoidable...

...like sharps and flats. Depending on the tonic, most major or minor scales contain sharps or flats (but never both). Since scales and keys are directly related, they share the same sharps or flats. There are two exceptions: C major and A minor have no sharps or flats. (Yay!)

Sign in, please...

A **key signature** appears at the beginning of a piece of music (and every subsequent staff). This tells you two important things:

 Notes that are played as sharps or flats throughout the piece

 The song's key

For example, the key of G major contains F♯, so its key signature will have one sharp on the F line. This tells you to play all F notes as F♯ (unless you see a natural sign ♮ in front of an F note, of course).

23

Let's look at a few common scales and keys...

Key of C
We've been working with this scale for a while, so it should be familiar. It has no sharps or flats.

36 The First Noel

☞ NOTE: Since the key of C major contains no sharps or flats, it looks as though there is no key signature.

24

Key of F

The key of F major has one flat: Bb. The scale form we're using here is in open position (mostly), but it's different than our C major scale in that the lowest note in the form is not the tonic. The tonic note, F, is actually on string 2. You'll find that, depending on the range of a particular melody, sometimes this form—with the tonic on string 2—will be better suited. Note that we'll reach up with our pinky for one high D note at fret 5 in this song.

37 America

Key of G

The key of G major has one sharp: F#. The scale form we'll use here is a moveable form of the open F major scale we just learned—we're simply moving everything up two frets to play it in the key of G.

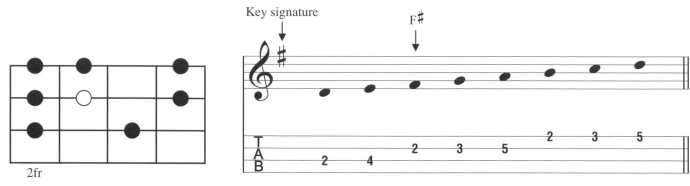

Key signature

F#

2fr

38 I've Been Ukeing on the Railroad

LESSON 4
Finger-pickin' good...

Up until now, we've been strumming through our chords, which sounds great. But there's another whole world out there to explore: **fingerpicking**! This technique will add a whole new dimension to your ukulele skills—and who doesn't love new dimensions?

Instead of brushing through all the strings with our strumming finger, we'll be plucking certain notes of the chord with our thumb, index, middle and ring fingers. Let's look at the basic idea.

First, get your plucking hand ready by planting your thumb on string 4, index on string 3, middle on string 2, and ring on string 1. Your thumb should be ahead of your fingers along the strings—i.e., closer to the nut.

Let's try a simple fingerpicking exercise using C and G chords. In the music, we'll indicate the plucking-hand fingers as follows: T = thumb, I = index, M = middle, R = ring. For the final C chord, just brush through the strings with your thumb.

🎵39 Clear as a Bell

Great! Let's try going in both directions now, using F and Bb chords. Remember your key signature—those are Bb notes in there!

🎵40 Floating Downstream

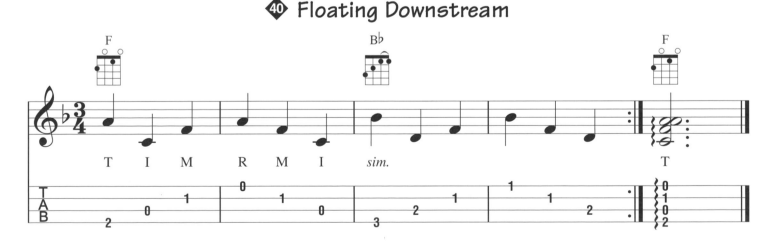

☞ NOTE: In these fingerpicking examples, you want all the notes to ring out. So, even though the tab only shows one note at a time, it's implied that you should be fretting and holding down the full chord.

There's a word for that...

The term for what we're doing—i.e., playing chords one note at a time—is **arpeggio**. It's basically a fancy way of saying "broken chord." There are nearly limitless arpeggio patterns that can be played on the uke. Some use all four plucking fingers, while others use only three. The cool thing is that, due to the uke's tuning, fingerpicking patterns sound especially unique on the instrument when compared to a guitar, for example.

Let's check out some more patterns. How about a new meter while we're at it? (You can multi-task, right?) In **6/8 meter**, there are six beats per measure, and the eighth note is counted as one beat. However, the first and fourth notes are stressed, so it's kind of like two slower pulses of three notes: **1**-2-3-**4**-5-6, **1**-2-3-**4**-5-6, etc.

In this example, we're using our thumb for strings 3 and 4 and assigning our index and middle fingers to strings 2 and 1, respectively. The thumb is moving back and forth between string 3 and string 4, which is a common fingerpicking technique.

41 Bluesy Arpeggio

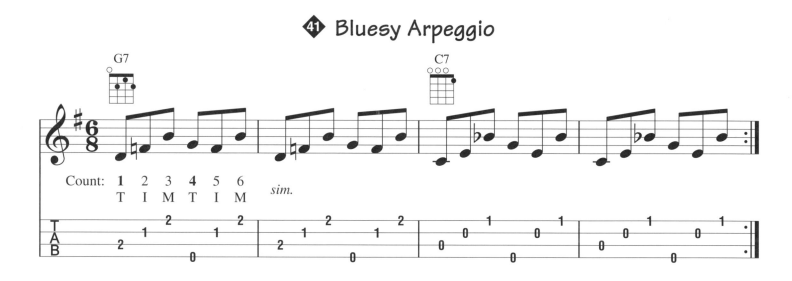

Here's a variation on the previous idea. This one is in the key of A major, which has three sharps: F#, C# and G#.

42 A Minor Variation

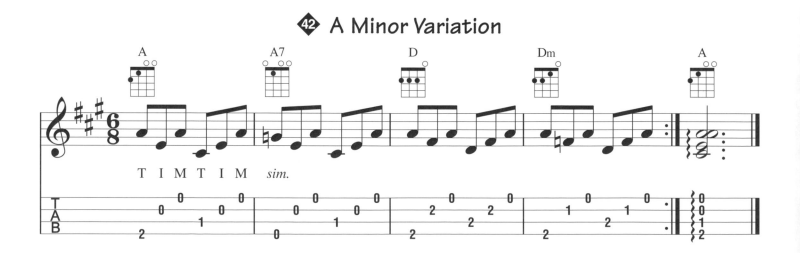

28

A little fancier...

Ready to learn a few more fancy chords? You've already learned several dominant seventh chords (and you make them sound good!), but there are other types of seventh chords, too. We'll look now at two other common types: **major seventh (maj7)** and **minor seventh (m7)**.

Cmaj7 Chord

While dominant sevenths sound bluesy or funky, major sevenths sound lush and pretty. Cmaj7 is a simple, one-finger chord that sounds great.

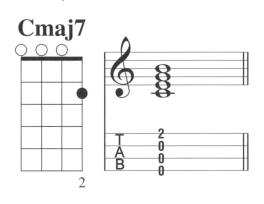

Gmaj7 Chord

For Gmaj7, just barre your index finger at fret 2 on strings 3–1. Ahhhh, that's nice!

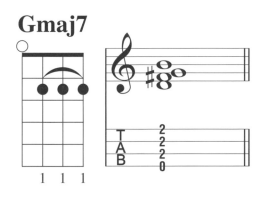

B♭maj7 Chord

This one is actually easier than the regular B♭ chord because you don't have to barre at all. Just leave that first string open!

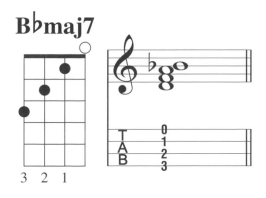

Let's jam...

Now, let's put those major seventh chords to good use. Listen to how beautiful the Bᵇmaj7 chord sounds in this fingerpicking pattern, which is in the key of D minor.

43 Music Box

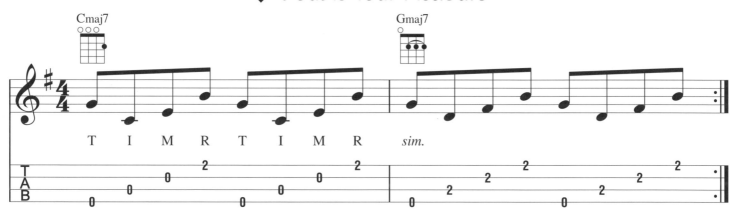

Double Your Pleasure

44 Double Your Pleasure

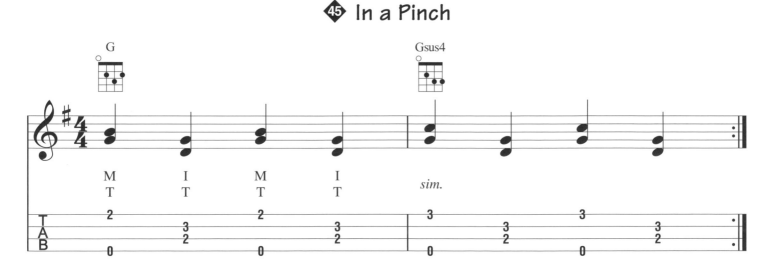

Don't pinch me!

Another great fingerpicking technique is called the **pinch** (but it won't hurt, we promise). This simply involves plucking a note with your thumb along with another finger at the same time. Try it out here with G and Gsus4 chords. Your index and middle fingers will remain on strings 2 and 1, respectively, while your thumb alternates between string 4 and 3.

45 In a Pinch

Major seventh chords are sometimes inserted between a major chord and a dominant seventh. In the next example, we have C–Cmaj7–C7, which leads nicely to F. Watch the plucking-hand fingering; it's very similar to what you just played.

46 Pinch Me, I'm Dreaming

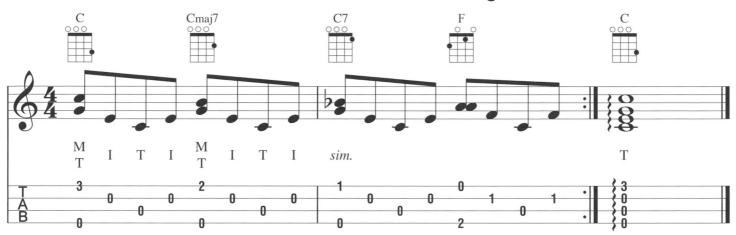

Time for some minor seventh chords...

Am7 Chord

Minor seventh chords sound a bit more complex or jazzy than regular minor chords. And it doesn't get easier than this one, folks. Am7 requires... no fingers at all!

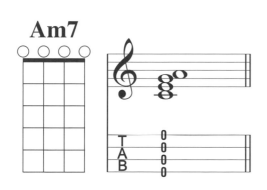

Em7 Chord

Here's a great-sounding chord that looks (and sounds) a bit like an incomplete G chord.

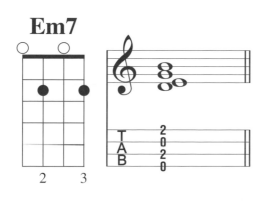

Dm7 Chord

This beautiful chord is a bit trickier because it uses all four fingers. The good news is that this voicing is already moveable (it contains no open strings), so once you get the hang of it, you can slide it up and down the neck to play other minor seventh chords. More bang for your buck!

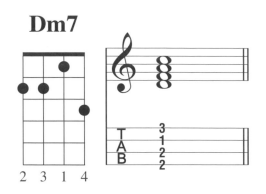

Gm7 Chord

This one is similar to a Gm chord, but with a little partial barre added.

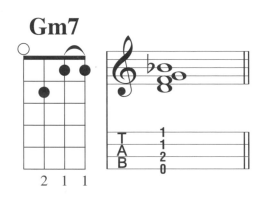

Let's jam out with some minor sevenths now...

You'll find that the alternating thumb trick is quite common in fingerpicking. Here are a few more ideas in that regard. Always pay attention to the plucking-hand fingerings shown. This one is in the key of Gm, which has two flats: Bb and Eb. (Notice the natural sign used in measure 3 and 4 for the C major chord.)

47 The Minor Seventh Dance

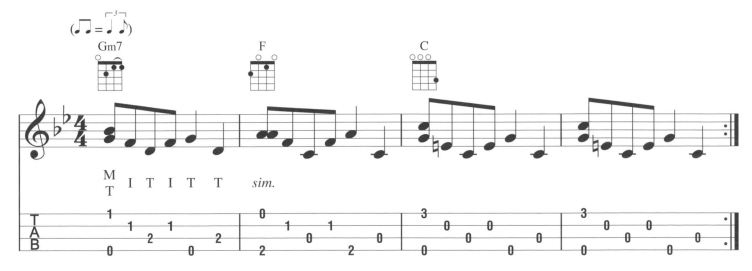

You can also pluck simultaneously with two (or more) fingers, with or without the thumb.

48 Classically-Tinged

LESSON 5
Got (More) Rhythm?

It's time to add to our rhythmic vocabulary. After all, the world isn't made up of just eighth notes and quarter notes!

What do you do if want to play faster than eighth notes without speeding up the tempo? You play **16th notes**, naturally! They have two flags or beams:

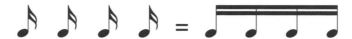

A 16th rest looks like an eighth rest but with two flags:

More math (easy math, though)...
Two 16th notes equal one eighth (just like fractions), and four 16ths equal one quarter.

To count 16ths, divide the beat into four parts by saying, "1 e & a, 2 e & a," etc.

1 e & a 2 e & a 3 e & a 4 e & a

Listen to track 50 to hear this new, faster rhythm. Note that we're playing all downstrums on the eighth notes. This is because we'll need to double up for the 16th notes that follow. By playing the eighth notes with downstrums, our hand will already be moving fast enough for the 16th notes. We only need to add the upstrums in between.

50 Progressively Faster

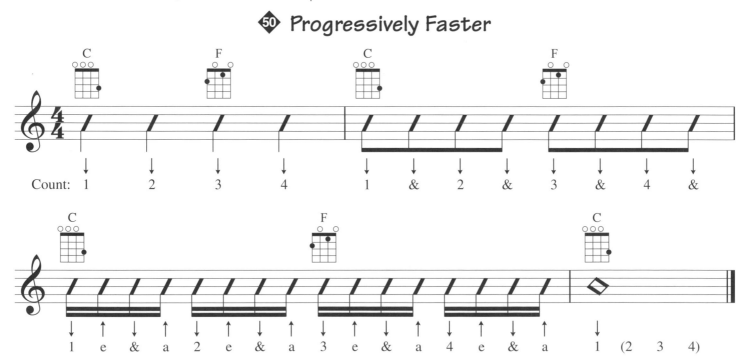

Try playing the above example yourself. Remember to play slowly at first and speed up only as it becomes easier.

34

Let's jam now...

Be sure to watch the strumming directions in these examples. We'll be mixing quarters, eighths and 16ths.

🔶51 Stop and Go

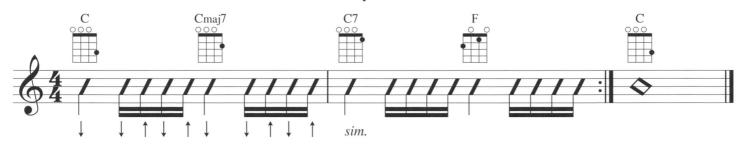

🔶52 Big Uke Rock

Watch out for the rhythm in this next one. It's a bit tricky!

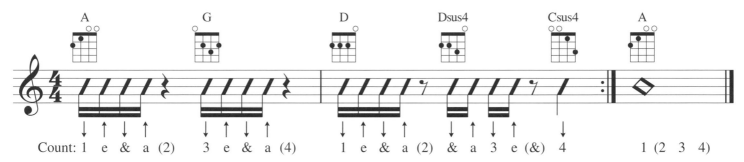

Count: 1 e & a (2)   3 e & a (4)   1 e & a (2) & a 3 e (&) 4   1 (2 3 4)

Nice and steady...

It's common to use alternating downstrums and upstrums when playing 16th notes. However, when playing a rhythm that mixes eighth notes and 16th notes regularly, you should keep your strumming hand moving **down** on every eighth note. This way, you can simply add in the upstrums when needed to create the 16ths. For example, instead of this, which is awkward and inconsistent:

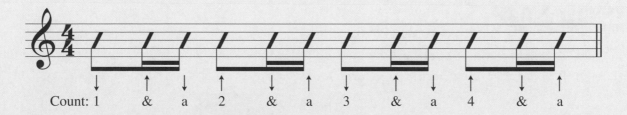

Count: 1   &   a   2   &   a   3   &   a   4   &   a

Keep your hand moving in steady eighth notes, like this:

This particular rhythm—one eighth followed by two 16ths—is quite common and is often referred to as a "gallop." Try it out!

53 Gallopin' on the Uke

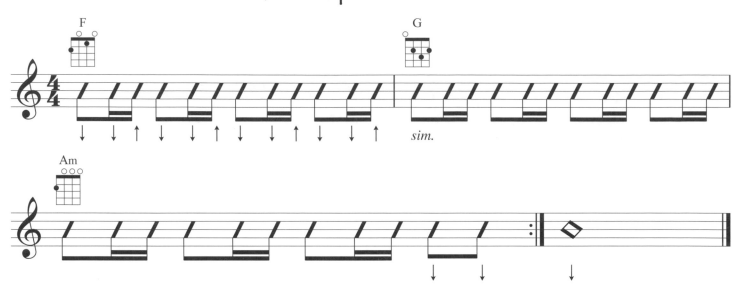

54 Riding the Rhythmic Waves

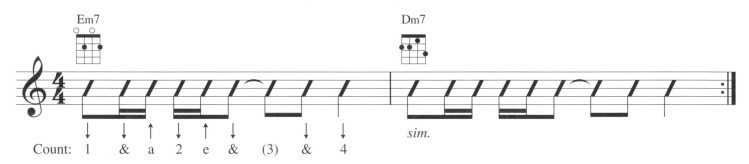

Count: 1 & a 2 e & (3) & 4

MORE CHORDS
Ready to add a few more chords to your bag of tricks? Then let's do it!

Aadd9 Chord

An "add9" chord is a major chord with an added note. It sounds a bit more sophisticated than a regular major chord. To play Aadd9, just add your ring finger to the A chord on string 1 at fret 2.

Aadd9

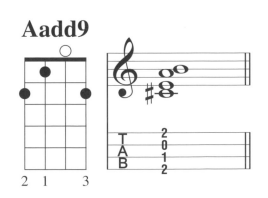

Fadd9 Chord

The Fadd9 chord is even easier than the F chord—it only needs one finger!

Fadd9

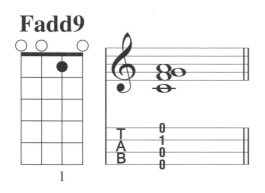

Cadd9 Chord

For Cadd9, add your first finger to the C chord at fret 2, string 3.

Cadd9

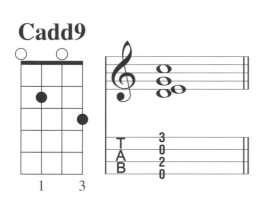

Let's see how these chords sound in action:

55 Everything Adds Up

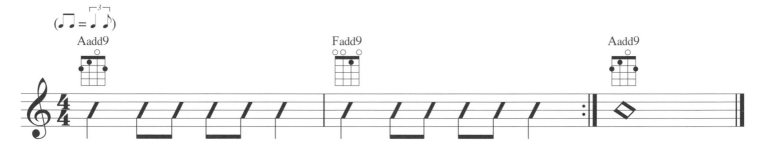

We can add 16ths to our 6/8 strums as well!

56 Adding the Final Touches

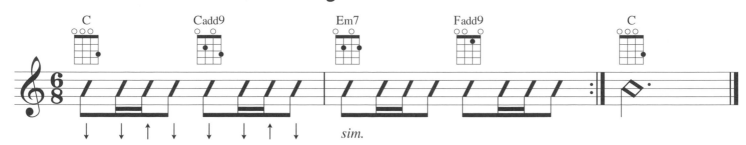

37

Add9 chords sound beautiful in fingerpicking patterns, too!

57 ◆ Add9 Arpeggios

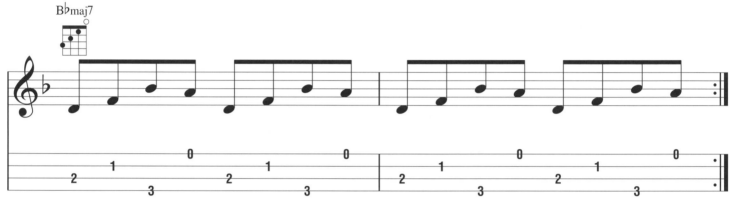

58 ◆ More Add9 Arpeggios

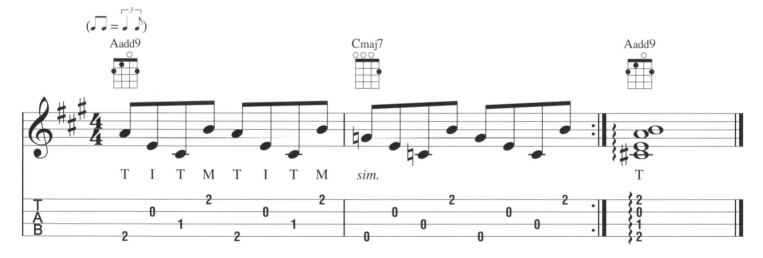

☞ TIP! Keep your eye out for common tones between chords to help you make the chord changes easier. In "More Add9 Arpeggios," for example, your ring finger is already on fret 2, string 1 for the Aadd9 chord. That means you can keep it there for both chords. Just remove your index and middle fingers for Cmaj7.

THREE TIMES THE FUN

You've already learned about the shuffle feel, which sounds like lopsided eighth notes. But did you know that the shuffle is actually based on a different rhythm called a **triplet**? (Feel free to impress your friends with that tidbit.)

Triplets

By now, you should know that two eighths equal one quarter note, and four eighths equal one half note, right? Guess what? It's also possible to play three eighth notes in the duration of one quarter-note beat. That's called an **eighth-note triplet**.

A triplet is beamed together with the number "3":

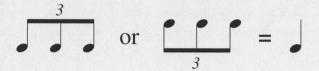

To count a triplet, say the word "tri-pl-et" as three syllables during one beat. Tap your foot to the beat and count aloud as you listen to track 59:

59 Tri-pl-et

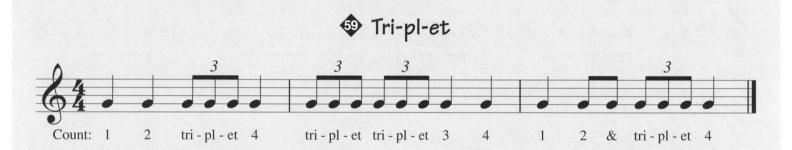

Ready for an "ah-hah" moment?

The shuffle rhythm involves playing the first and last notes of a triplet. That's why the first eighth note is longer than the second—twice as long, to be exact!

Try out your new triplet rhythm in the next two examples.

60 Triplet March

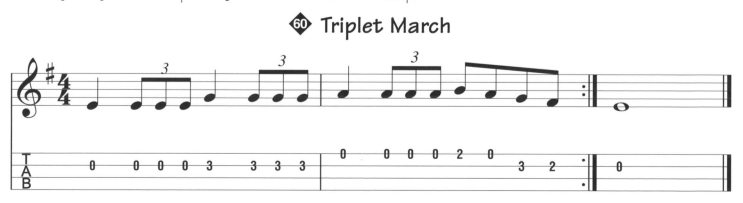

 61 Bluesy Triplets

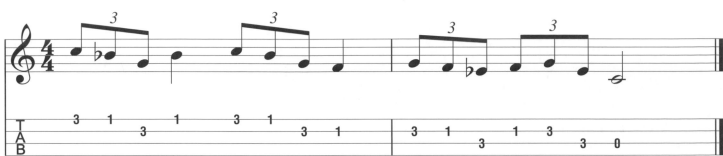

Let's try strumming some triplets...

Strumming triplets can be tricky. At slower tempos, you can usually strum down-up-down, down-up-down, etc. and get by just fine. This is a good technique because it pairs the downbeat with a downstrum, which is generally more accented than an upstrum by default.

62 Strummin' Triplet Style

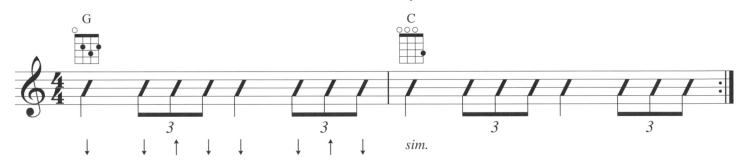

A bit faster...

When the tempo creeps up, however, using down-up-down for every beat gets harder and harder, so we need to find a better method. One way is to simply alternate strokes and do our best to accent the beat even when it lands on an upstrum: **down**-up-down, **up**-down-up, **down**-up-down, **up**-down-up. That approach sounds like this:

63 Alternating Triplets

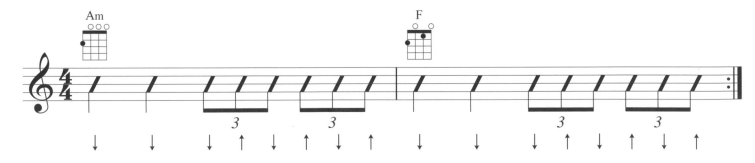

It works, but it's harder to accent the beat without a good, strong downstrum. Fortunately, there's another way...

The triplet strum...

Alternatively, you can use a **triplet strum**. There are several variations of a triplet strum, but they all involve combining index-finger strums with thumb strums. Here's a common one:

 1 Strum down normally (with the index finger).

2 Strum up with the thumb (it's really more of a flick of the thumb).

3 Strum up with the index finger.

This brings you back around to start the pattern over again with an index-finger downstrum on the beat. You just have to remember that, when you strum up with the thumb, your index finger still needs to remain below the strings so it can follow with an upstrum of its own.

Listen to the previous example, this time played with the triplet strum described above. In the music, a "T" is shown below the upstrum marks when it's used.

64 Triplet Strum

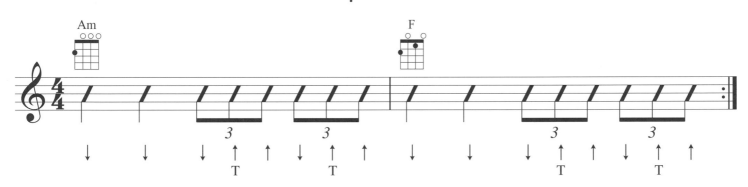

This sounds a little more natural, because you have those strong downstrums paired with the downbeats. You can certainly use straight alternating strums if you prefer, but give the triplet strum a try and see how you like it!

65 Down and Back Up

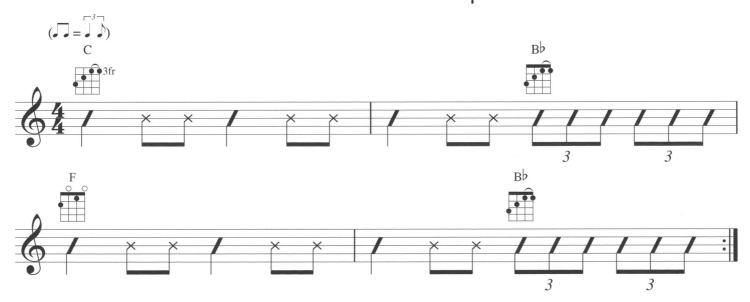

LESSON 6
Let's get fancy...

You've been quite patient while learning your chords, rhythms, scales and strums. As a reward, we'll give you a few "tricks of the trade"—some **slur techniques** that you may have heard about.

Slur techniques (or "legato," if you prefer the Italian) allow you to play more than one note with each pluck. In other words, you can pluck the string once and then "slur" two (or more!) notes, resulting in a smooth, flowing sound. Let's look at the three most common slur techniques...

66 Slide

Looks like this:

Just like the name implies, play the first note by plucking the string, then sound the second by sliding your fret-hand finger up or down on the same string. The second note is not plucked, so you get two notes for the price of one! In the music, a curved line connecting two notes indicates a slur. A diagonal line indicates the slide.

Now, let's try it out in some riffs...

67 Up and Back

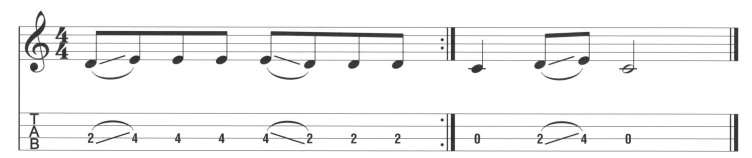

68 Bluesy Slides

It takes a little time to get the hang of it, so go easy on yourself!

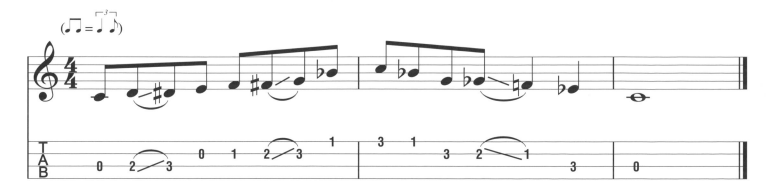

69 Hammer-on

Looks like this:

Pluck the first note and then use another finger as a "hammer" to press down a higher-pitched note on the same string. Be sure to use enough force for the second note to sound!

70 Worried Rock

71 Pull-off

Looks like this:

This is kind of the opposite of the hammer-on. In other words, pluck the first note and then tug or "pull" the note off the string to sound the lower note. If the lower pitch is fretted as well, you need to have both notes fretted when you pluck the first note.

72 We're All Pullin' for You

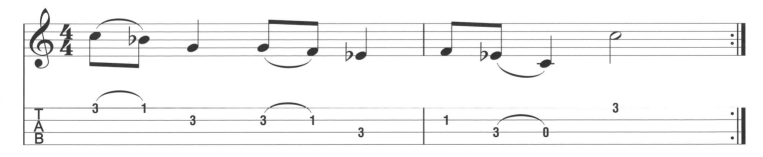

LESSON 7
Strike up the band...

As in the first book, this isn't a lesson...it's a jam session!

All the other **FastTrack®** books (Guitar, Bass, Keyboard, Drums, etc.) have the same two songs featured at the end of the book. This way, you can either play by yourself with the audio or form a band with your friends.

☞ ONE LAST THING: When you see "D.S. al Coda," jump back to this symbol 𝄋 and play until you see "To Coda." At that point, skip ahead to the Coda, which is marked with this symbol ⊕.

Basement Jam

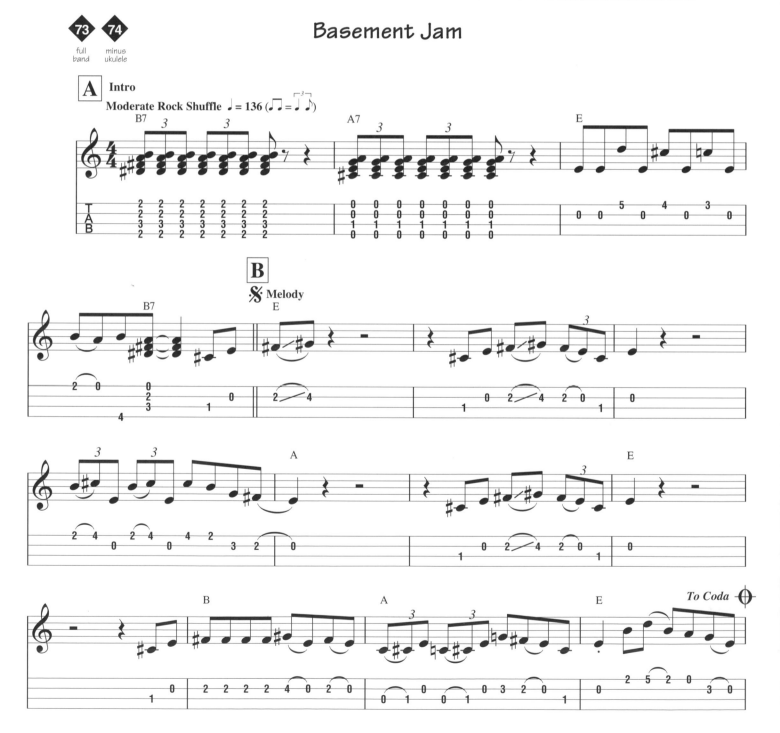

Dim the Lights

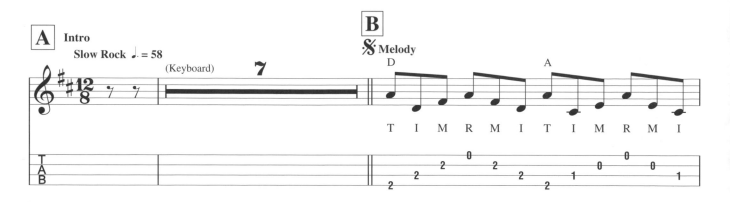

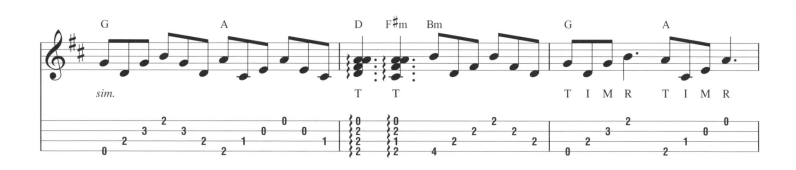

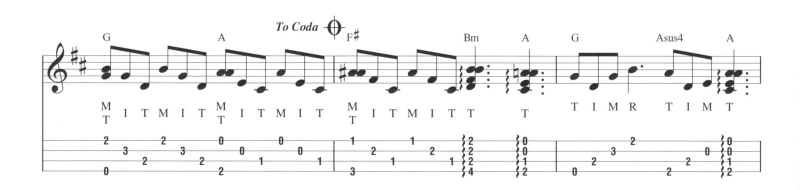

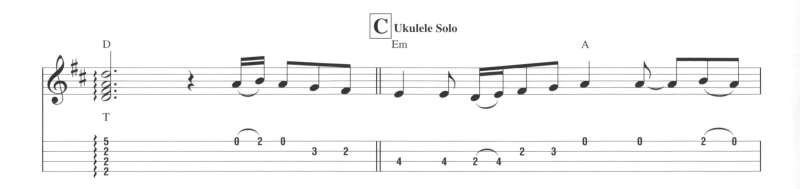

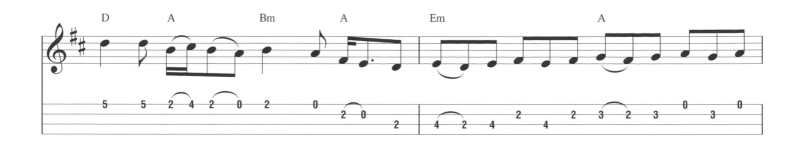

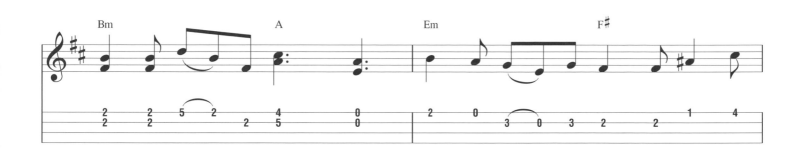

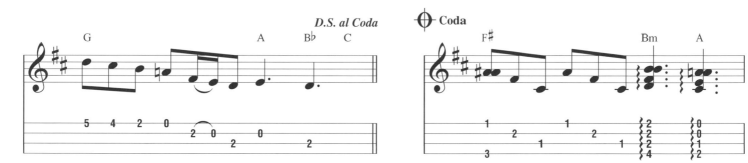
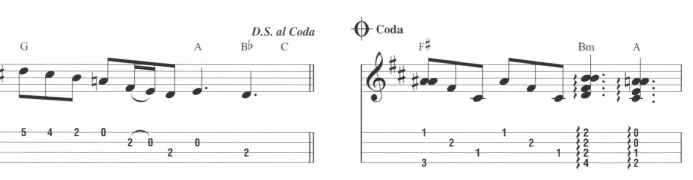

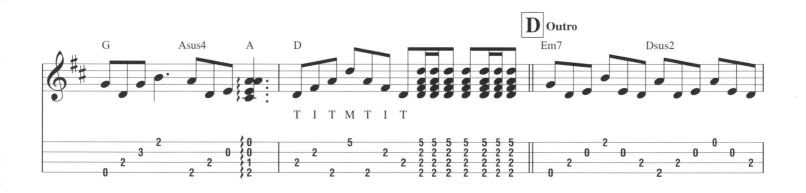

SONG INDEX

(...gotta have one!)